Bucklebury in Focus

Photographers: Jo Andreae and June Dutton

Edited by Christine Storey, Wynne Frankum
and Sheila Kent

Foreword by Cecilia Millson

Published by
Bucklebury Parish Council
on behalf of the
Bucklebury Millennium Committee
1999

Published 1999

ISBN 0-9536139-09

Printed in Great Britain by
Biddles Ltd., Book Manufacturers,
Guildford, Surrey

Contents

Acknowledgements

We are very much aware that this book is the result of the considerable effort and support of a large number of people and in many ways it is their book as well as ours. Without their help and the loan of their photographs this book would not have been written. We would like to thank:

Janet, Reg and Jason Allum
Sheila Annetts
Eric Baker
Mr K. Bartholomew
Elaine and Chris Baxter
D. Botherel
Miss I. Brooks
Bucklebury & Marlston Women's Institute
Ethel Cruse
Major J. Dunlop
Miss O. Edwards
Molly and Doug Eggleton
Martin and Sue Fidler
Neville Gosling
Margaret Grannum
David Green
Sylvia Haines
Jean Hardy
Rupert Hartley Russell
Willy Hartley Russell
Mrs S. Hawkins
Jimmy Henwood
Malcolm and Joan Hynes
Mollie and Norman Jaques
Sherree Johnson
Debbie and Jerry Kent
Mrs P. King
Mrs N. Lambert
June Lawes
Gillian and Cyril Lewington
Alistair MacOran-Campbell
Barbara and Peter Mann
Joan Martin
Alfreda and Arthur Matthews
Alan Renaut
Graham Renaut
Jackie and Neil Rendall
Dora Parker
Elsie Paulin
Joe Paulin
Brockhurst School
Geoff Stocker
Phyllis May
June Miles
Cecilia Millson
Helen Relf
Alan Robinson
Gerry Sanderson
Francie Smee
Audrey Summersby
Joan and Roy Tench
David Tipton
Beccy Ward
Mr and Mrs J. Watts
Mr L. Watts
Mr and Mrs F. Welch
Robert Wells
Geoff Whatley
Bill Young

We have also included photographs published in the Newbury Weekly News, by photographers unknown to the editors.

We are very grateful to a number of organisations and businesses for their support:
Donnington Trust for their considerable financial assistance
T4 Cameras for discounted photographic materials
Lockside Software Ltd for the loan of a Macintosh computer system.

We particularly thank Cecilia Millson for her historical expertise, Sue Hopson for supplying and dating some of the postcards and Erica Tipton for helping with sales. The editors offer a special thanks to their long suffering husbands Roger Frankum, Ron Kent and Malcolm Storey. We would also like to thank all those people who allowed themselves to be photographed.

Finally we apologise if we have inadvertently omitted anyone.

Foreword

It is probable that the 20th century has seen more changes in the life style of men and women in this country than any other in the past millennium.

As the pages of this book are turned it will be realised how much Bucklebury has been affected by these changes. Thanks to the inspiration and diligence of Wynne Frankum, Sheila Kent and Christine Storey we now have this collection of photographs of various aspects of village life.

The photographs themselves bear witness to the progress which has been made during the century. The original photographers would be amazed by the reproduction of their work by modern technology.

However one thing has not changed, the enthusiasm with which the people of Bucklebury celebrate local and national events. The celebrations taking place to welcome the new millennium, in which this book plays an important role, are indeed worthy of Bucklebury's historic heritage.

Cecilia Millson, 1999.

About the photographers

Jo Andreae lives in Upper Bucklebury. After travelling the world taking many remarkable photographs, Jo gave up her job as a business analyst to run her own business, "One World One Camera". Her love of architecture and her artistic eye enable her to produce memorable images of buildings and the countryside. Since starting her business in January 1999, she has rapidly gained a reputation for her photographic work and greetings cards.

June Dutton started with exotic wildlife photography, then qualified in photography at Newbury College. She is now mainly a portrait photographer who also reports on events in this area for the Newbury Weekly News. Apart from her pictures, she has also made a valuable contribution to the book through her experience of handling pictures both photographically and digitally. Her enthusiasm for the latter has been very useful and greatly appreciated.

About the editors

Christine Storey has lived in Bucklebury for 10 years. She is a founder member of the Bucklebury History Group and the Bucklebury Heathlands Conservation Group. Her expertise in the computing field has enabled her not only to repair digitally some of the damaged old photographs but also to produce this book from home.

Wynne Frankum has lived in Bucklebury since 1972 and takes a keen interest in local history. From a career in teaching she has now specialised in educational history focusing on the Victorian era. Over the years she has been involved in numerous parish organisations and is at present a Parish Councillor.

Sheila Kent is the only one of the group who is Bucklebury born, as were numerous generations of her family. Having lived here practically all her life she is very knowledgeable about Bucklebury people and places. Her great love of Bucklebury and especially the Common made her a willing founder member of the History Group. Her knowledge and enthusiasm have been invaluable in the compilation of this book.

The Village

The village is the historical heart of the parish. The church, manor and foundry nestle in the valley of the River Pang which was a source of power for hundreds of years. There were water powered wheels for the farms at River Barn and Black Barn as well as at the old foundry in the village.

In 1736 the Hedges family was running a blacksmiths on the site of the foundry which employed up to 20 people. Farmers and cottagers took pots, pans and metal implements to be mended.

The King brothers took over from the Hedges family and added furnaces for iron casting. The foundry became a big employer in the area. In 1946 they were producing iron, brass and aluminium castings for agricultural machinery as well as road gratings, man hole covers and meter boxes for Newbury Corporation. Many are still in use. A round gas meter cover can still be seen outside the main Newbury post office.

The Whatley brothers took the foundry over in 1946 and ran it until it closed in 1986. Many of the contributors to this book remember being drawn to the foundry as children to watch the daily activity.

Jo Andreae

1999

An early picture of the riverside cottages.

Bucklebury Foundry

The open top car in this picture took foundry workers to do jobs further afield. c1908.

Mr King and his sons fitting a red hot iron tyre to a wagon wheel, about the turn of the century.

The foundry workers in the 1890's.

From left to right. Top row: M.G. Davis, J. Lake, I. Franklin, J.G. Wyles
Second Row: Mr Patey, J. Lloyd, T. Franklin, W. Britton, R. Brown, G. Butler, F. Freeman
Third row: C. Fisher, D.W. King with I. Hedges on his knee, W. Sellwood, Mr Hawkins, W. Sellwood, I. Jacobs.
Bottom row; A. Sellwood, young H. Hedges and T. Sellwood.

Jo Andreae

Iron grave memorials can still be seen in Bucklebury.

The foundry water wheel.

Go-carts for sale.

Go-carts and Gyro-planes

The foundry started making go-carts in 1959. A couple of years later they diversified further, designing and producing machinery for making concrete blocks.

In 1960, Geoff and his brother pursued their mounting interest in gyro-planes. Later Geoff helped a local firm in the production of gyro-planes including test flying and pilot training. Other local enthusiasts made up the Bucklebury Gyro Group. They trained on various machines including this B7 at the end of a tow rope.

Gyro-glider being towed.

Cut Your Costs by Fitting This Cutter Bar

to your

Land Rover

Land Rover with the Mower in working position.
"Farmers' Weekly" photo.
(See other side for Transport position).

NOTE THESE POINTS:

- STANDARD 5 FOOT CUTTER BAR OF LATEST DESIGN.
- EASILY ATTACHED. NO EXTRA HOLES TO DRILL.
- CUTTER BAR DETACHED BY REMOVING 2 BOLTS AND A PIN ONLY
- GROUND CLEARANCE NOT AFFECTED WITH CUTTER BAR DETACHED.
- HIGH, SELF-LOCKING LIFT. NO RATCHETS OR PAWLS TO WEAR.
- LIFT GEAR DOES NOT PUT ANY EXTRA WEIGHT ON THE VEHICLE'S SPRINGS.
- V BELT DRIVE TO CRANKWHEEL ENSURES SAFETY FOR KNIFE.
- TOTALLY ENCLOSED BALL BEARINGS IN CRANKWHEEL.
- ECONOMICAL AND EFFICIENT IN USE.
- THISTLE CUTTING CARRIED OUT WITH TRANSFER BOX IN HIGH GEAR.

FOR FURTHER PARTICULARS APPLY TO THE MANUFACTURERS:

WHATLEY BROS. : BUCKLEBURY

READING, BERKS.

In the early 1950's the Whatley brothers, then owners of the foundry, designed and built this grass mower attachment for Land Rovers. Some of these were exported.

The old carpenter's shop on the left was rented to sheet metal workers when this photograph was taken in the 1970's.

Jo Andreae

The Foundry House as it is today. It is still a family home.

Part of the foundry before it was demolished.

These are the houses built on the site of the foundry. A horse's skeleton was found under the floor when the buildings were demolished.

St Mary's Church

The church of St Mary the Virgin is an ancient building of chalk and flint, lovingly cared for by parishioners. The original small church has been added to over the centuries and contains much of interest, including the Norman south doorway. One of the Millennium projects is the restoration of the striking mechanism of the clock.

St Mary's Church with Glebe Cottages to the left. c1908

Jo Andreae

The same view today.

View from the field behind the church c1930.

This is Mr George Davis who was tower captain from 1875-1925. He lived in the Old Post Office as did his son.

Jo Andreae

The Norman archway in 1999

The Old Post Office. c1906

June Dutton

The back view of the Old Post Office in 1999.

Winter 1995

Glebe Cottages earlier this century.

The Nativity and Passion plays

The angels appearing to the shepherds.

"Is there any room at the Inn?"

The Three Kings offering gifts to baby Jesus.

The Nativity and Passion plays were started by Jean Hardy, wife of Rev. W.D.Hardy. The first plays were performed at the Old Manor theatre (Bucklebury House) before moving to the church. People came from far and wide, in coaches and cars, to the numerous performances that were held over two weekends.

A large cast of players and singers came from surrounding villages to take part.

The plays ceased when Rev. and Mrs Hardy left the parish in 1958.

Peter's denial. 1950

The church and its people

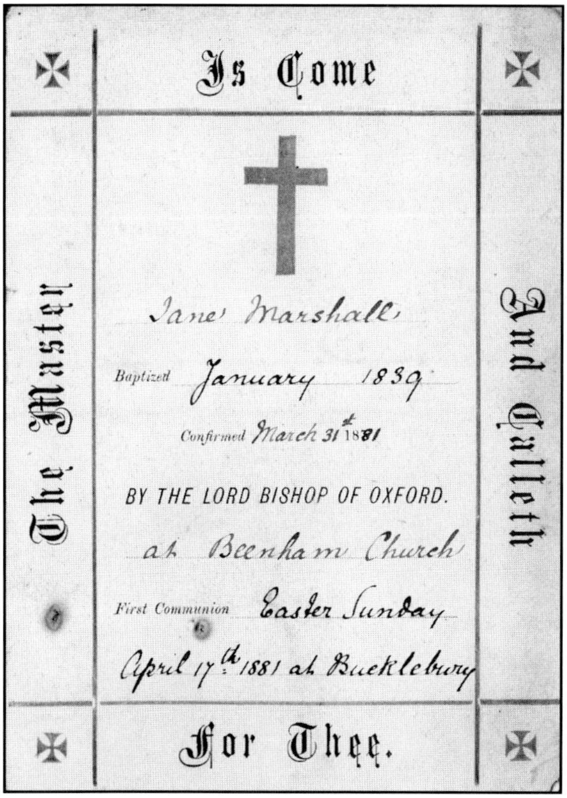

The Master Is Come And Calleth For Thee.

Jane Marshall

Baptized January 1839

Confirmed March 31st 1881

BY THE LORD BISHOP OF OXFORD.

at Beenham Church

First Communion Easter Sunday

April 17th 1881 at Bucklebury

A Confirmation certificate belonging to Mrs Sheila Kent's great grand-mother. She was confirmed after she married.

Jo Andreae

Time flies.
The famous fly window in the church.

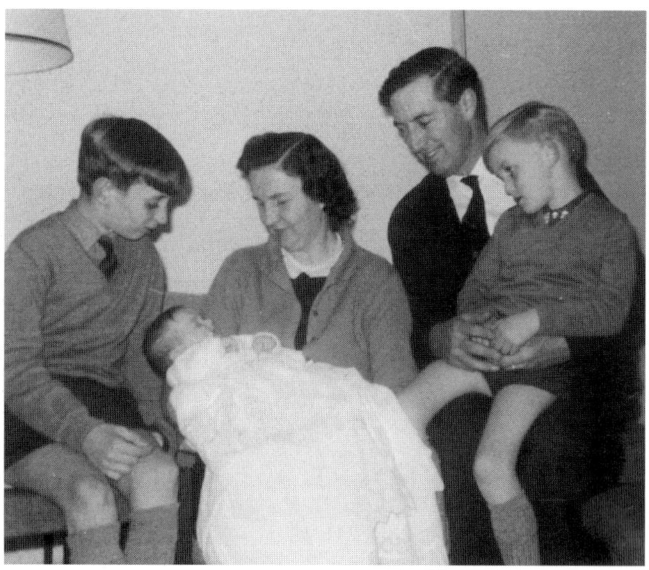

A christening in the Kent family, in 1967. The christening robe is a family heirloom.

Ethel Lucy Dean married John Barrett. 1908

Ethel was driven to St Mary's Church in this carriage by her father, Alfred Dean, on her wedding day. Alfred was coachman at the Manor.

Esther Mathews married Stanley Brown in 1937.

Joan Carr married Malcolm Hynes in 1964.

Deborah Fidler married Jeremy Kent in 1983. The 1st Thatcham Scouts formed a guard of honour.

C.J.Willoughby

Bindi Jaques married Alan Davies in 1994

Before electric lights arrived. c1930

Jo Andreae

The service at the end of the Milleflora weekend in June 1999. There was a flower festival in the church, gardens were open in the parish and refreshments served in the Victory room. The Milleflora was the first event to celebrate the Millennium and raise money for further activities.

June Dutton

Brownie parade. 1997

June Dutton

The women's branch of the Royal British Legion parade every year for the Remembrance Sunday service at St Mary's. They are pictured here in 1997.

June Dutton

Debbie Kent and Judy Holmes dressing the font for harvest festival in 1998. On Oct. 12th 1947, the harvest festival service was broadcast by the BBC to New Zealand.

June Dutton

Ringers in 1999. From back left corner: Ros Durham, Alastair Campbell, Tim Durham, Jack Durham (the current tower captain), Anne Ryder, Angela Smith, Natasha Durham and Reg Allum.

Jo Andreae

The Old Vicarage.

The vicar of Bucklebury originally lived at Glebe Cottages but in the early 18th century this vicarage was built. It is now a private family home.

The Victory Room and Recreation Grounds

The Victory Room was erected after the First World War and has been used for village functions ever since. Money to run it is raised by the Victory Room Social Club.

A Victory Room Social Club event in 1998.

The cake stall at the fête on 8th May 1995 at the Victory Room and recreation ground. The fête commemorated the 50th anniversary of Victory in Europe.

Jo Andreae

The play area in 1999 with play equipment and safety surfaces.

June Dutton

Some of the Bucklebury cricket team about to leave for an away match in 1999. The cricket pitch used to be on the green at the Blade Bone.

Bucklebury Football Teams

There used to be two football clubs in the parish. Bucklebury Common Football Club played at the Blade Bone and amalgamated with Bucklebury Village Football Club after the Second World War. Bucklebury Village Football Club was started in 1926.

The Bucklebury Common Football Club in 1938-39.

The Bucklebury Village Football Club in 1949-50.

The party to celebrate a good year, 1979-80: Division 2 winners, All Champions Challenge Cup winners, League cup winners, Giant Killers Trophy and Reserves Division 3 winners.

The IMS Bucklebury F.C. 1997-98 season Div. I. Champions Newbury D&D Sunday League.

The River Pang and Bucklebury Ford

Jo Andreae

Sun lighting the River Pang looking west from Rushden's Farm, in 1999.

Crossing the ford yesterday ...

Jo Andreae

and today.

Generations of Bucklebury children have enjoyed the delights of the River Pang on a hot summer's day.

Christine and Rodney Mann, May 1955

Early 1960's

Jo Andreae

1998

Jo Andreae

Taking a short-cut through the ford. 1998.

Jo Andreae

"Messing about in the river."

Farming

The pig farm is now a feature of the Pang Valley. It was started 15 years ago by Gordon Munro-Ashman. The pigs are reared outdoors for the welfare friendly market. Eight hundred sows produce 17,000 piglets per year.

Jo Andreae

A field of pigs in 1998.

June Dutton

A farm walk for pig breeders followed by tea at the Victory Room, spring 1999.

Jo Andreae

A view across the Pang valley from Hopgood's Green Road in 1998. Ford End is in the middle of the picture.

Jo Andreae

A maize harvester loading maize into a trailer, summer 1998.

Neville Gosling *del.*

The Black Barn, on the north bank of the Pang, east of Bucklebury village, before the fire in the 1990's. This barn was latterly used for storing hay for Mr Munro-Ashman's pigs. The barn belongs to the Bucklebury Estate.

Jo Andreae

The Black barn in 1998, after fire.

Bucklebury House

The first Manor House in Bucklebury was built by the Abbot of Reading in the 12th century. John Winchcombe rebuilt it in 1540.

Bucklebury Manor before it was burnt down.

Bucklebury House is now also referred to as the Old Manor. Bucklebury Cottage, just up the hill, was renamed The Manor in 1906. This photograph shows the buildings of Bucklebury House including the 15th century dovecote.

Jo Andreae

Bucklebury House in its lovely setting, home to Miranda and Willie Hartley Russell and their three children. 1999

A pageant of the history of Bucklebury was held in June 1977 to celebrate the Queen's Silver Jubilee. This scene shows Elizabeth 1st with her courtiers visiting Bucklebury Manor. The pageant took place around one of the fish ponds in the grounds of Bucklebury House.

Bucklebury Home Guard 1940-45.

During the second world war Captain Dunlop was in charge of the Bucklebury Home Guard. Henry Hartley Russell was second in command. They met at the Old Manor, Bucklebury House, to train and had a parade most Sundays. They played an active role in the early part of the war. Their job was to guard against German paratroopers. They kept the night watch in the area. Bucklebury also had a Special Police force during the war.

From left to right. Back row: Edwards, May, Simpson, Sellwood, Rolfe, Fife, unknown, unknown, Rosier. Second Row: Neate, Morton, Parker, Herbert, Dr Brodribb, Farrant, Mulsen, Harding, Holmes, White, Green. Third Row: Nailor, Hale, Caslin, Harris, Dunlop, Hartley Russell, Rawson, Johnson, Lewis, Guard. Front row: Wells, Fisher, Marchant, Froude, Millson, Harvey, Appleton.

War and the Matthews family

Henry Matthews and his wife Edith, George Lailey's sister, photographed in 1918.

Henry and his brother William served on the same gun throughout the First World War. Henry and Edith had four children, Harold, Mary, Arthur and Betty.

Harold is shown in his Chief Petty Officer's uniform in 1944/45. This photograph of Mary was taken when she was a Petty Officer in the W.R.N.S. in 1946. Arthur's photograph was taken in 1944 when he was a trooper in the Reconnaissance Corps.

By chance, Arthur met his brother in Bombay just as the Japanese surrendered.

Bucklebury Farm Park

Bucklebury Farm Park was opened in 1992 and is a very popular local family attraction. It is run by Rupert Hartley Russell, pictured here with his children, Jemima and Henry, in 1999.

June Dutton

Jo Andreae

A tractor ride in 1998.

Feeding some of the many young animals. 1998

A great attraction for the young. 1998

The old school

There had been a school in Bucklebury for local children since early in the 19th century. In 1870 it became a legal requirement to provide a school place for every child and so a larger school was needed. This building was built in 1874 for 170 children.

June Dutton

As it is in 1999, converted to a family home.

Mr Davis, Headmaster 1909-1912, with Miss Jane Waite standing, and from left to right, Miss Stella Davis, Miss M.Sellwood and Mrs Davis.

A class in the 1920's.

The scholars of 1920.

A great effort was made to dress smartly for a school photograph. Some children even had to borrow boots. This picture was taken about 1918.

The class of 1930. This was Arthur Matthews first day at school. His elder brother, Harold, and sister, Mary, are also in this picture along with Miss Giles and Mr Cleaves.

Pounds and Common gates

The Browns lived in this house at Brown's Gate opposite the brick pound. The house was burnt down sometime in the 1940's. Only the centre chimney was left and was incorporated into the new house.

Brown's Gate cottage before it was burnt down.

Jo Andreae

Brown's Gate cottage in 1999.

Straying animals were put into the pound to be collected by their owners. A small charge was made when they were collected. c1908

Jo Andreae

The brick pound in 1999.

Nuttage Gate. Children were often given a penny to open the common gates for vehicles.

Nuttage Gate Cottages when the posts of the Common gate were still visible.

Jo Andreae

Nuttage Gate in 1999.

Mrs Edith Wigmore in Nuttage Gate Cottage.

Past occupants of Nuttage Gate

Mrs Edith Wigmore moved to Nuttage Gate after marrying Archie Wigmore. She was a founder member of the Bucklebury and Marlston Women's Institute and was the first National Savings officer when the WI joined the scheme. She was also a founder member of the Bucklebury and District Women's Section of the Royal British Legion. Edith died in 1980.

Mr Archie Wigmore (d.1989) worked as a gardener and was a well known exhibitor at the flower shows.

Mr Archie Wigmore in the early 1980's.

Hillfoot

Hillfoot with the track to Hillfoot Farm on the right.

June Dutton

The first four council houses were built at Hillfoot in the 1930's. Two more were added later. They are now mostly privately owned. This photograph was taken in 1999.

Chapel Row and The Blade Bone

The 13th century chapel gave its name to the area from the top of the hill to the end of the row, where the post office is now. It is thought to have been called the chapel of St Mary Magdalen and had reached a sad state of repair by 1634. Little is known of this painting. Did the chapel really look like this or is it an artist's impression?

Many remember two particularly severe winters in the 1940's. At the end of January 1940 rain fell while the temperature was below freezing, icing over everything. Many tree boughs bent or broke and these telegraph wires, at the top of Chapel Row Hill, were severely stretched. 1947 is remembered for virtually no school from Christmas to Easter.

Iced wires at the top of Chapel Row Hill.

Jo Andreae

Homestead, now called Barfield, Chapel Row in 1998.

In the middle distance is Chapel Row Pond, with a flock of sheep. c1908

March 1976. Mrs Mary Thomas (Bucklebury and Marlston Women's Institute president) and Mrs Noel Rand (Bucklebury and Marlston Horticultural Society president) planting trees at Chapel Row Pond. Horticultural Society work parties cared for the pond.

This pond, opposite the Old Bake House, is no longer here. c 1927

Jo Andreae

The Old Bake House, Chapel Row, in 1999.

The road looking north west towards Chapel Row Hill.

This line of oaks used to continue down Chapel Row Hill towards Bucklebury House. People can remember some being cut down and they were certainly gone by 1945.

Chapel Row shop and Post Office

Chapel Row shop and Post Office was originally a cow shed. Ron Dennis, as a young lad on his way home from school, used to bring the cows from the field behind these cottages and chain them up in the cow shed ready for milking.

Mrs Johnson bought the small holding in 1929 and opened a shop and post office. Reg and Janet Allum ran the shop and post office from 1966 until they retired a few years ago.

Chapel Row shop and Post Office c1950.

June Dutton

Taken in 1998.

June Dutton

Inside the Chapel Row shop in 1999.

Chapel Row Fair

The Reading Mercury, 8th July, 1816, advertised the fair to be held on 29.8.1816 "for hiring servants, buying and selling cattle and other merchandise and for the encouragement of gentlemen gamesters will be given by the Lord of the Manor, a purse of five guineas to be played for at cudgels. The person that breaks most heads to have the purse; the blood to run one inch, otherwise deemed no head and for the second best man will be a gold laced hat. Two shillings a head will be given to the person that breaks the first twelve heads; likewise a good hat to be wrestled for, a donkey race for a new bride, and a jingling match and sundry other diversions."

Chapel Row still has a fair at the end of August but thankfully it is very different now.

Jo Andreae

Chapel Row Fair in 1999.

The Blade Bone Inn

Janet Allum can remember the building to the left being used for dances. Just visible behind the second car, is a petrol pump. The sign "Strange and Sons' Aldermaston" advertises the brewery which went out of business in 1929. Pale ales, stout, wines, spirits, luncheon and teas are listed. This photograph was taken about 1930.

Jo Andreae

The Blade Bone Inn today.

June Dutton

Buying a pint.

June Dutton

Pool in the Blade Bone's public bar in 1999.

The Blade Bone Inn was a terminus for buses from Reading and Newbury. The WI recorded that in 1965 the Blade Bone to Reading bus ran once every hour and to Newbury once every two hours. The fares were 2s 6d single to Reading and 1s 8d single to Newbury. Buses went from the Slade and the Village to Newbury every Thursday, market day, and Saturday. There were, at one time, three tea shops as well as the Inn providing refreshment for the travellers.

Many still remember Mr Lock, the bus conductor, from the 1940's. There was a single decker bus shed, called the dormy, next to the Blade Bone Inn where Mr Dean, the driver, used to store the bus at night. The old surgery was built on this site.

The words on the side of this earlier bus, above the Thames Valley sign, are difficult to read but on the original clearly start with "Reading" and end with "Bucklebury Common".

c1930. Now Orchard House, just west of the Blade Bone Inn.

c1927. The Misses Thatcher's tea room, Green Gardens, was in the house on the left of this view. They served Sunday lunches as well as teas. After the war they moved away to run a hotel.

Martin and Sue Fidler had owned the Blade Bone Butchers shop for 21 years on 18th February 1999. It has been a butcher's shop since at least the end of the Second World War.

Fourteen years ago offices were built and 6 years ago, in 1993, another storey added, turning it into a house. The Fidler family moved into their new home from Stanford Dingley.

The butchers supply meat far and wide and their products are taken all over the world by satisfied customers to give as presents, even pork sausages to Israel.

It is not unknown for the phone to ring on Christmas day with delighted Americans thanking the Fidlers for the Christmas morning treat of the magnificent sausages they've just enjoyed.

June Dutton

The Blade Bone Butchery in 1999.

June Dutton

Inside the shop in 1999.

June Dutton

George Wells and Barry Snell binding hay at the Chapel Row dairy when it was a working small-holding.

George and Bob Wells at the Chapel Row dairy. The back of council houses can be seen. 1960's.

Ploughing the land for vegetables at Chapel Row dairy.

Memories of wartime bartering include exchanging a bit of bacon for stale bread from the baker to feed the pig. The family pig is often referred to when remembering life in Bucklebury during and between the wars.

For those on the Common, keeping the pig warm during winter started early. Having marked out a patch of bracken a few days before, cutting was carried out on 1st September, and not before. One of its uses was as animal bedding and sometimes as an insulating layer, lining the inside of the pig-sty. The bracken was stored in ricks which were sometimes thatched.

Cutting bracken.

Avenue House was an estate worker's cottage built in the early 1700's. It is to be found at the top of Hatch Lane.

The same house in the 1960's or 70's. Since this photograph was taken Avenue House has been extended again and a porch built on the front.

Jo Andreae

A 1960's house in Hatch Close in 1999. Some of Hatch Close was built on water meadows.

Jo Andreae

The 1950's houses in Paradise Way photographed in 1999. At the bottom of Paradise Way were the Paradise Cottages, now converted to one home.

June Dutton

Ann and Steve Athawes with their two sons watching sport on TV.

Jo Andreae

Shepherd's Heath, another modern Bucklebury residence, taken in 1998.

The Avenue

The Avenue early in the 20th century. Bicycles and riders are leaning against the front of Chapel Row stores.

The view of the road looking west. Paradise Lane and the Green are on the left of the picture. c1908

These are the cottages that once stood where Donnington Close is now. They were demolished in 1969.

The Donnington Hospital Trust

The Donnington Hospital Trust has existed since the original licence to create the foundation was granted by Richard II in 1393 to Richard Abberbury, Knight, who held the Manor of Donnington. After the War of the Roses in 1485 Donnington Manor and Hospital passed to the Crown. In 1632 it was bought by John Packer, whose great-grandson Robert married Mary Winchcombe, heiress to the Bucklebury Estates. This family worked to restore the resources of the Trust throughout the 17th century, and it is now into its fourth century of benevolent concern.

Willie Hartley Russell is the current patron and chairman of the trustees. The trust now has 50 alms-houses in Bucklebury, Donnington and Iffley in Oxford.

More of the Trust's fascinating history can be found in Cecilia Millson's book *The History of Donnington Hospital*.

Jo Andreae

Donnington Close was built by The Donnington Trust in 1970. This photograph was taken in 1998.

The site of the current doctors' surgery with Winchcombe Lodge in the background.

Dr. Munro-Ashman joined the Aldermaston practice after the Second World War. He set up his own surgery at Oaklea in The Avenue before leaving in the 1960's to specialise in dermatology. Dr. Raban took over the practice and had the surgery built next to the Blade Bone Inn. This bungalow is now a private residence. The new surgery was opened in 1993.

Jo Andreae

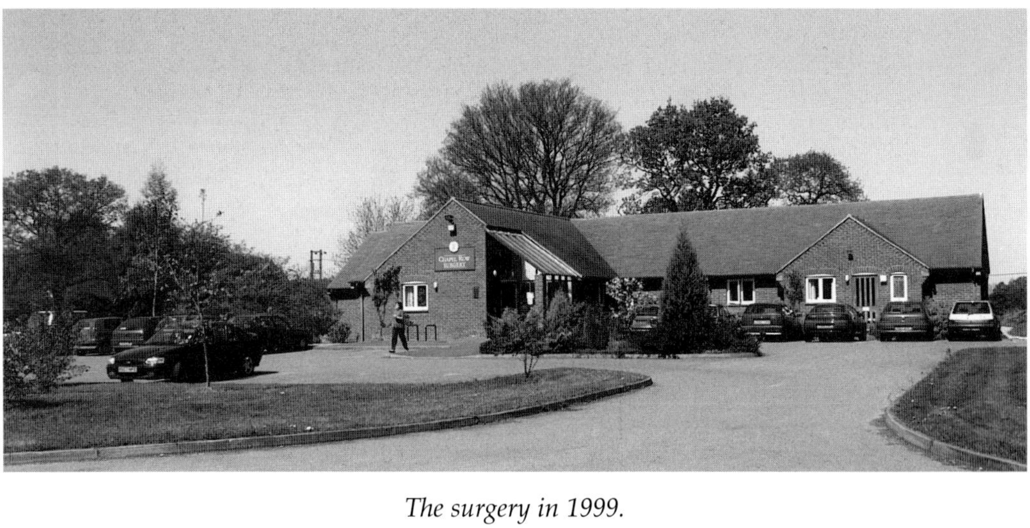

The surgery in 1999.

Jo Andreae

The pharmacy at the surgery in 1999.

The Chapel Row liaison group was set up in 1995 to help local people with information about health and social care. There are two meetings a year held in one of the villages covered by the group: Aldermaston, Beenham, Bradfield, Brimpton, Bucklebury, Midgham and Woolhampton. Below is Jan Hayward, the chairman of the group, on the left, with four speakers at one of the informal meetings.

June Dutton

The Chapel Row liaison group in 1998.

June Dutton

The right hand cottage of this pair was, earlier this century, Miss Snell's Refreshment Rooms. This delightful building below, at the end of its drive was a stable. Spring 1999.

June Dutton

The Black Barns, by "Shingleton's", are no longer here. c1930

Wood Gate, at the Bradfield end of the Avenue. c1930

The Common

The first crossroads on the Common, east of Upper Bucklebury, showing one of the Victorian clumps of Scots pine planted in 1902 in memory of Queen Victoria. Tomlins is just out of view on the right. This picture was taken c1928.

In the past, grazing animals kept down the vegetation on the acid soil of the Common. This picture shows a later time when trees were beginning to take hold.

During the second World War the army took over part of the Common, bulldozing the top soil into large mounds, which can still be seen to the south of the road. The Common was used for living quarters and to store vehicles.

June Dutton

Consideration shown to other residents in the post box in Cox's Lane outside Tomlins.

These pictures were taken in 1956 on the south side of the Common, opposite Angel's Corner.

In the background is one of the mounds of top soil left by the army. There is still little sign of the dense birch scrub we see now. Gorse, heather and bracken are remembered as the dominant ground cover.

The coppiced gorse, or furze, was harvested within living memory by the Paulin family of The Slade, to supply wood for the manufacture of parasol and umbrella handles.

Some say the birch scrub grew up quickly after a major fire in 1938/39. Others also remember it growing up after the army left.

Ice on the Common with the top soil mound in the background.

Taking advantage of the winter's cold weather. From left to right: Nicholas Dunlop, Nicky Perry, Clair Perry and Sarah Dunlop.

Bucklebury Heathlands Conservation Group clearing birch scrub from the Common to encourage heather to grow and the nightjar to breed. There have been other local groups, as well as the Estate, clearing the Common over the years.

June Dutton

Keeping the cold out with Bucklebury punch. Feb 14th 1999.

Bucklebury Punch Recipe

From the Newbury Bee Keepers

This punch tastes very like a red wine based mulled wine. It is robust enough to be left simmering on the ashes for hours.

For 60 people take:
5 litres orange juice
2 litres red grape juice
600ml bottle Ribena
450gms honey (or less if you don't have a sweet tooth)
3-5 sliced oranges
1 sliced lemon
2 cinnamon sticks
2-3 tsp cloves
4tsp ground ginger
4tsp ground allspice
1 litre water-dilute to taste

Gently bring to the boil, stirring to dissolve the honey, then simmer.

The Cemetery

The cemetery was opened in 1885 and it was later enlarged. For many years the chapel was regularly used for services until All Saints Church was built.

Jo Andreae

Angel's Corner

The name Angel's Corner appears on the Manor Court rolls in 1699.

Angel's Corner is owned by the Brooks family and the hut was built as their weekend retreat away from the bustle of Newbury. It is rented to the scouts at a peppercorn rent.

Miss Brooks remembers the land being wet enough to grow a willow copse and having sundews, an insectivorous bog plant, underfoot.

June Dutton

The scout hut, Angel's Corner, in 1998.

June Dutton

Inside the scout hut in 1999.

There is a story that if locals could put up a house in a day and have smoke rising from the chimney by evening, they could live in it. This may explain why so many old cottages nestle in hollows on the Common.

This cottage near Vanners barn was burnt down in the 1940's.

The two cottages in Osgood's Gully in 1940. Major Dunlop bought them in 1951. They were extended and modernised making the attractive house we see today.

Osgood's Gully

Osgood's Gully copse was planted about 120 years ago on the fields whose old boundaries can still be seen. The copse was to provide wood for local industry, both locally and in Thatcham. Alder was grown for brush heads, ash for the handles, hazel for pea sticks and willow for basket making.

Here we see Hubert Fairchild, right, with his father-in-law at Osgood's Gully in 1953.

Laying water pipes to Osgood's Gully in 1956-57. The supply was from the water tower at the main crossroads which provided water for the war time campsite on the Common.

Many households in Bucklebury had evacuees from London during the Second World War. Mrs Ada Mathews and her daughter Joan looked after 9 year old twin brothers from London, Ronald and Charles Hines, during October and November 1939.

Ronald and Charles having tea with the Mathews at Waven.

Mr Bartholomew's daughter, Sylvia, with cousin Deanna in 1947.

After the war some homeless families squatted in the army's vacated huts on the Common.

The Bartholmew family lived here after Mr E. Bartholomew was demobbed from the RAF.

Vanners Barn

Vanners Barn belonged to the manor and was rented out this century to local farmers. It was used for storing hay and straw. In the early 1900's wagons brought the Sunday school children to the barn for their annual tea party. The barn was rethatched in the 1950s, then had a corrugated iron roof, before being burnt down in 1985.

In the past celebrations of every important event, particularly coronations, took place in the barn.

The newly thatched barn.

On this very old oak is a plaque telling us that to celebrate the coronation of Edward VII in 1903, 1,200 people assembled and a service was held by the Rev. Hope Gill followed by a picnic with refreshments served in Vanners Barn.

Here is Nicholas Dunlop climbing the Coronation Oak in 1953.

Jo Andreae

View from the Common towards Sadgrove Farm in 1998.

Jo Andreae

Malcolm Hynes tending his bees at Hop Pightle pasture, Sadgrove, in 1999.

Mr George Dance had a dairy herd at Sadgrove Farm and used to deliver his milk in the area. In the 1930's William Lailey, son of George Lailey's brother William, used to help deliver the milk in this cart, ladling the milk from a churn into cottagers' own vessels.

June Dutton

This is one of the two fish ponds on the Common dating back to the 12th century. Monks lived in Bucklebury and dug the ponds to provide fish for their table. There are also fish ponds in the grounds of Bucklebury House from the same era.

Briff Farm before the modern extensions.

Jo Andreae

Briff Farm in 1999.

June Dutton

Scotland, north west of Chapel Row

This area is more recently known and sign-posted as Scotland Corner. Two of these cottages were sold as a pair for £100 in the 1922 Bucklebury Estate sale. They each had a living room, sitting room, pantry, two bedrooms, wood-house and closet. A well supplied their water. This picture was taken in 1998.

This is St Saviour's Church, the iron church, c1930. It was situated just off The Avenue near Nine Elms and was demolished in 1972.

Bucklebury Place

Bucklebury Place was built by Mr Arthur W. Sutton in 1893, and he lived there until 1915. He was Senior Partner of Sutton's Seeds in Reading. He was a great horticulturalist and benefactor to the Parish.

The architect for the house was Frederick William Albury (d1912) of Reading. The building was originally set in about 236 acres, including surrounding farms, and a cricket field. After the departure of Mr Sutton, the house and gardens underwent many changes of ownership and use, including as a Red Cross convalescent home. Bucklebury Place is now in private ownership and is converted to apartments.

Mr Sutton also built the Fireside Club for parishioners use where many activities took place.

A touching reminder of the affection Mr Sutton had for the area was the fact that, in poor health, he retired to the south coast and named his house, Bucklebury.

Bucklebury Place residents during the Second World War.

Joan Astley, a local girl, was nursing at Bucklebury Place in 1942 when it had been turned into a Red Cross convalescent home for British troops wounded on active service.

Second from the left in the front row is the head cook, Miss Jaques, whose brother was the postman in Bucklebury for many years. Joan, third on the left, met her future husband Roy Tench when he was convalescing. They married at St Mary's Church and still live in Bucklebury.

Joan remembers that in late 1942 the home was taken over by the Czechoslovak Army for their soldiers in this country to convalesce while being treated at Park Prewitt Hospital, Basingstoke.

The back of Bucklebury Place at the end of the Second World War.

Jo Andreae

The main staircase and hall. Spring 1999

Country Sports

The Dunlop family came to live at Winchcombe Lodge in the mid 1920's. In 1932 Captain Dunlop leased the shooting rights for the whole Bucklebury estate and held the lease until his son took it over. Partridge and pheasant were shot throughout the winter, using local beaters. This photograph was taken at Bucklebury House.

Jo Andreae

The Garth and South Berkshire Hounds on 13th February 1999 at Carbins Wood.

June Dutton

Heatherview kennels, midmorning in 1999.

Hopgood's Green is a hamlet which has seen little change over the years. c1927

Upper Bucklebury

At the turn of the century Upper Bucklebury consisted of the Three Crowns public house, the cemetery and a few cottages. Only a few more houses were built until the late 1920's when Roundfield started to be developed and bungalows were built along the roads. Roundfield continued to expand, then in the 1960's much more building took place including the new school and houses in Berry's Road.

Pressure for houses in Upper Bucklebury continues and often one house is demolished for two or more to replace it. Of all the places in the parish, Upper Bucklebury has seen the most growth.

Broad Lane looking east towards Chapel Row, c1927.

The first bungalow on the left belonged to Mr Sid Sellwood. Further left, out of the picture, was the bungalow called Lyndhurst, built in 1924 by Billy Faithfull for Arthur Matthew's parents. Arthur, George Lailey's nephew, was born a year later.

Next to Sid Sellwood's bungalow, before the Second World War, was the home of the local undertaker, Mr W. Herman. The next house had a market garden at the rear.

The Memorial Hall

The Memorial Hall was built in memory of the men who died in the Second World War. A temporary hall, made from two army huts, was erected and fund raising began. The permanent building, our current hall, was officially opened on May 20th 1961. It cost £8000.

The members of the Bucklebury and Marlston Women's Institute outside the temporary hall in 1960, celebrating the 40th anniversary of the formation of the local branch.

Jo Andreae

This picture was taken in 1998.

Concrete play area in 1965.

Jo Andreae

The Memorial Hall playground in 1998.

Bucklebury Robins Juniors

This cycle club started in 1957. They went all over the country to race on cycle tracks. They cycled at the Hockett field and had a concrete circular track at the back of the Memorial Hall where children play football now. This club folded in 1965. In the picture, from left to right are Charlie Heavier, Steve Wooldridge, Norman Eggleton, Brian Clarke, Norman Unwin and Graham Renaut.

The tennis courts at the Memorial Hall. Bucklebury Tennis Club is currently run by Mike James. It is a popular club and maintains the courts to a good standard.

June Dutton

The mobile library makes regular visits to Chapel Row, the Village and the Memorial Hall.

June Dutton

June Dutton

Cycling home from work.

Inside the mobile library. 1999

The Bucklebury & Marlston Women's Institute

The history of Bucklebury in embroidery.

During 1961-62 the Bucklebury and Marlston Women's Institute embroidered this Tympanum depicting the history of Bucklebury. It was mounted in the Memorial Hall above the stage by Mr Alec Millson in September 1962.

Back row: Miss Alice Talbot, Mrs Dorothy Millson, Mrs Bisset
Front row: Mrs Keevil, Miss Davis, Mrs Maria Boyle

The design shows St Mary's Church flanked on either side by the Avenue of Oaks. The Cavalier on horseback is a reminder of the Civil War. George Lailey is shown bowl turning. There are two inhabitants taking part in a bloodthirsty cudgelling match at one of the Chapel Row fairs. The monks are fishing in the fish ponds and gypsies camp on the Common. The armorial bearings are those of the Winchcombe family.

Back row: Miss Smyley, Mrs Muriel Titcombe, Mrs Cecilia Millson, Miss Carden

Front row: Mrs Mary Dawson, Mrs Ella Westwater, Mrs Robbins

A WI jam-making centre in the garage of The Gables, Briff Lane when Alice Talbot lived there. The jam was made for the war effort. Quality control was strict and each pot had to be labelled with the cook's name. From left to right are: Mrs Hobbs, Mrs Gore, Miss Alsbury, Miss Talbot, Mrs Anido, Mrs Kennedy, Mrs Watkins, Mrs Fairchild and Miss Salway.

Jo Andreae

The WI in 1999.

A WI outing in 1937. The Bucklebury and Marlston WI was started in May 1920.

In 1965 the WI attended a garden party at Buckingham Palace celebrating the Golden Jubilee year of the Institutes. About 9000 women from England, Wales and the Channel Isles had tea with the Queen.

A WI float in 1978 Revels, raising funds for the village halls. Part of this year's fun was a reintroduction of back-swording. No blood was spilt, just burst ballons on top of protecctive head gear. Clive Wallace was the under sixteen champion .

Other groups using the Memorial Hall include the West Berkshire Ballet School which moved from Thatcham to the Memorial Hall in January 1998. It is run by Gillie Robinson.

The Bucklebury Players

For many years Bucklebury enjoyed a strong association with drama. Before and after the Second World War Mabel Ball and Henry (Bobbie) Wingett produced plays at the Old Manor theatre, by kind permission of the lord of the manor, Mr Henry Hartley Russell.

The Women's Institute drama group also contributed their share of good entertainment. After the death of Mrs Ball, followed shortly by that of Mr Wingett, a group of drama enthusiasts founded the Bucklebury Players in September 1958, with the result that two productions of three-act plays were performed every year at the Bucklebury Memorial Hall.

Unfortunately, with changing pastimes and commitments, membership dwindled until the company could no longer continue. Reluctantly, after forty happy years it was decided to disband the players in December 1998.

The Bucklebury Players. "The Importance of being Earnest" by Oscar Wilde in 1963. Paul Cheetham, Anne Watts, Patrick Dowling and Joyce Heywood.

Bucklebury & Marlston Horticultural Society

Mr Davis with his cups and certificates won at the horticultural shows.

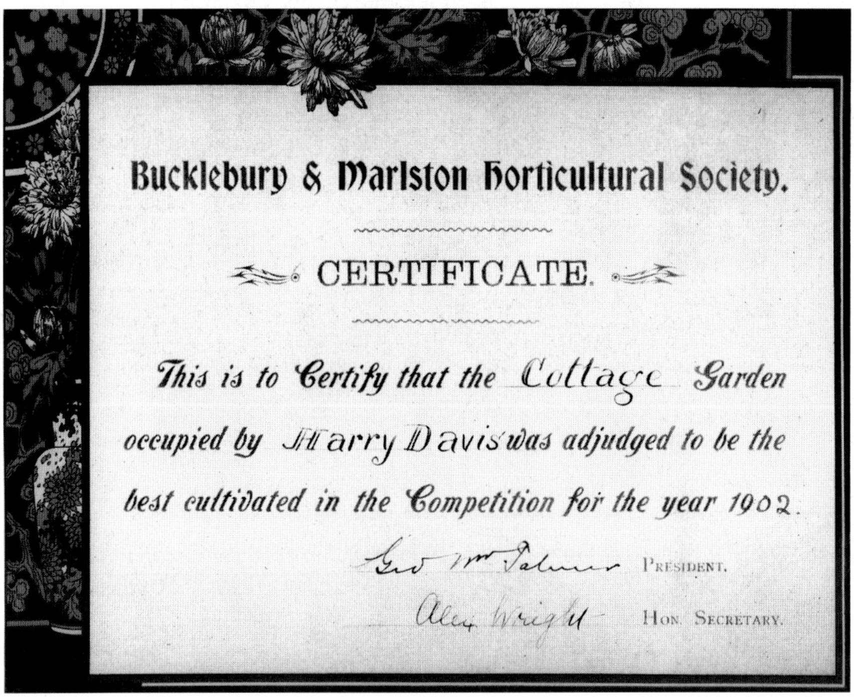

Bucklebury & Marlston Horticultural Society.

CERTIFICATE.

This is to Certify that the Cottage Garden occupied by Harry Davis was adjudged to be the best cultivated in the Competition for the year 1902.

Geo. Wm. Palmer PRESIDENT.

Alex Wright HON. SECRETARY.

One of the certificates from 1902.

Jimmy Henwood and Harry Copas won many cups and prizes for their vegetables and flowers at the shows. This picture was taken in 1963. The cup this time was won by Jimmy, seen on the left.

Fund raising events

June Dutton

The Royal British Legion Christmas sale in 1995 in the Memorial Hall. Mrs Judith Fleming, president, with Mr Eric Baker.

Jo Andreae

One of our photographers, Jo Andreae, at her stall for the Christmas fair in 1998.

Jo Andreae

Christmas fair, November 1998. The tympanum embroidered by the WI in 1961-2 is above the stage.

Jo Andreae

The first public consultation for the Bucklebury Vision Statement in 1998. This was a new venture for Bucklebury.

Bucklebury Play Group

Biscuits and juice time in the 1960s.

Summer 1982 with Gabriele West, Bridget Seward and Diane Dalgano.

June Dutton

Newbury's MP David Rendel was given a special responsibility for pre-school experience and visited the Bucklebury Pre-school group in 1999 at the start of his fact-finding tour.

1960s

Bucklebury Brownies were started by Mrs Price in the 1960s. Later, they folded but were restarted by Brownie Wilkins in 1974 and has been going ever since. Mrs June Lawes ran it for 10 years. The current leader is Mrs Ros Durham, who presides over a pack of 26 enthusiastic girls.

June Dutton

The Bucklebury Brownie pack on an enrolment night in 1999.

June Dutton

The changing face of Broad Lane

Jo Andreae

Windows being replaced by the original style windows in early 1999.

Jo Andreae

New clay tiles being laid in Broad Lane, late 1998.

The Millsons have lived in Bucklebury for generations. Robert Millson (1839-1924) was one of 11 brothers and one sister and all were enthusiastic cricketers. With so many siblings they were able to form their own cricket team, playing at the Blade Bone with their sister scoring for them.

Robert first married Sarah Tidbury who unfortunately died soon after bearing their third child, Chandos, who also died. Sarah's sister, Emily, moved to Tidmarsh, where Robert worked on Alec Hopkins' estate, to look after the two remaining children, Sarah and Harry. Robert later married Emily and they had six more children, Albert, Arthur, Edmund, Archibald, Ada and Kate (Sheila Kent's grandmother).

The Millson family had considerable influence on the house building in Upper Bucklebury.

Mr Robert Millson is in the middle.

Robert built the houses on the triangle known as Mount Pleasant for himself and some of his children. He also built Cherry Tree cottage, pictured in the inset, near Zin Zan, for another child. In the main picture you can see Mount Pleasant, the first house he built.

This house was built by a different Mr Millson for his daughter, Doris, when she married Hubert Fairchild. Here they are seen in the garden with a cousin, Kathleen Millson. This house was demolished in the mid 1990's and replaced with the two new houses, numbers 7 and 9 Broad Lane.

Shops and Garage

Peach's Store and garage c1927.

The store was opened by Tom Peach and his wife in the 1920's. Tom later mended bicycles and this part of the business developed into the garage. The entrance to Long Grove can be seen on the left.

A later picture of Peach's Store and Post Office. Arthur Matthews remembers buying sweets as a boy from the front room before the right hand extension was built and became the shop.

In between times.

Jo Andreae

Peach's Garage in 1998.

June Dutton

A separate shop was built in the 1970's after Muriel Watts (née Peach) died. Peach's Store is now owned by Mr and Mrs Shingadia who took over from Mr and Mrs Fernandes in 1998.

Jo Andreae

Besides selling provisions the shop is a post office and newsagent.

Mr Fernadez, the previous owner, at the post office counter.

Mr Shingadia selling a lottery ticket to a customer.

Jo Andreae

June Dutton

Quality Fayre is the other general store in Upper Bucklebury. Maurice Bull took it over in June 1994. These pictures were taken in 1998.

Jo Andreae

June Dutton

In 1965 the WI noted various food prices:

Bread 1s $3^{1}/_{2}$d large loaf	Tea 7s to 9s per lb
Butter 3s 8d per lb	Coffee 8s per lb
Cheese 3s 4d to 4s 8d per lb	Eggs 5s per doz.
Milk 10d to $11^{1}/_{2}$d pint	Petrol 4s 7d to 5s 6d gallon

Jo Andreae

Everyday life in Upper Bucklebury

June Dutton

Gardening in May 1999

Jo Andreae

The Postman. August 1999

In early 1999 residents were given the option of having water meters fitted to measure the consumption of water used per household. Many took advantage of this.

Jo Andreae

Digging a hole so that water meters could be fitted. Berry's Road in spring 1999.

Jo Andreae

The new water meter.

Bucklebury is not connected to the mains gas supply. Houses are heated today by either solid fuel, electricity, oil or calor gas.

Jo Andreae

A delivery of coal in Mr Barrett's lorry. 1999.

Jo Andreae

An oil delivery in Burden's Heath

Jo Andreae

Calor gas being delivered.

Jo Andreae

The delivery of fresh milk to our homes has been a tradition for many years. Now it is only delivered 3 days a week in Bucklebury. Cheaper milk sold in nearby supermarkets is a threat to this service.

Jo Andreae

Delivering the morning papers.

There are a couple of free local newspapers delivered each week to all houses: the Newbury and Thatcham Chronicle and the Reading Chronicle. Peach's Stores also arranges the delivery of daily newspapers.

Jo Andreae

The public telephone box.

Jo Andreae

The ice cream van in 1998.

The chimes of the ice cream van herald a summer treat for the children. Children of the 1940's bought their ice cream from a man on a bicycle.

Jo Andreae

Refuse collection, Monday morning, 1998. Wheelie bins replaced dustbins in the 1990's.

Jo Andreae

1999. Collecting paper, glass, tins and rags for recycling. This is a relatively new service.

Jo Andreae

Christmas lights in Berry's Road in December 1998.

Jo Andreae

Teachers Rachel and Chris Ward with their twin sons have swapped jobs and houses with Jenny and Ian Stevenson and their two children from Melbourne, Australia, for a year. Here are Jenny and Ian cooking dinner in 1999.

Jo Andreae

Sunday roast, consisting of chicken, roast potatoes, carrots, peas and gravy, with the Tilley family, Briff Well, Little Lane.

Jo Andreae

Hallowe'en 1998. The children are playing "trick-or-treat" in Berry's Road.

Jo Andreae

Roller blading in Berry's Road

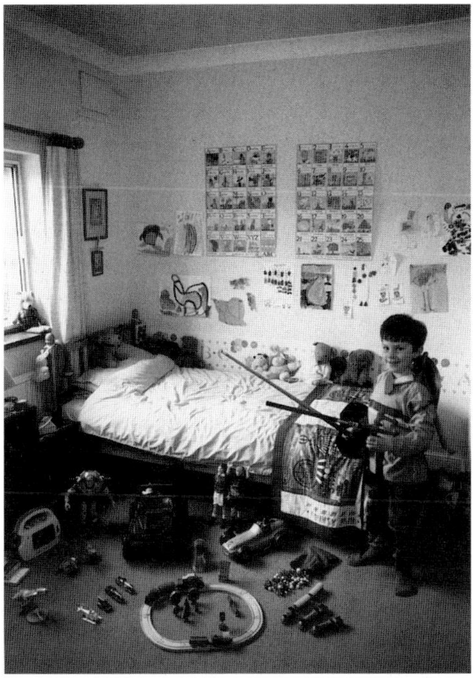

Jo Andreae

Digby Coulson with a selection of his toys including "My first Sony tape recorder" and "Thomas the Tank engine".

Digby in his bedroom at Byles Green.

Jo Andreae

Digby riding his bike.

Washing on a line in Bucklebury.

Jo Andreae

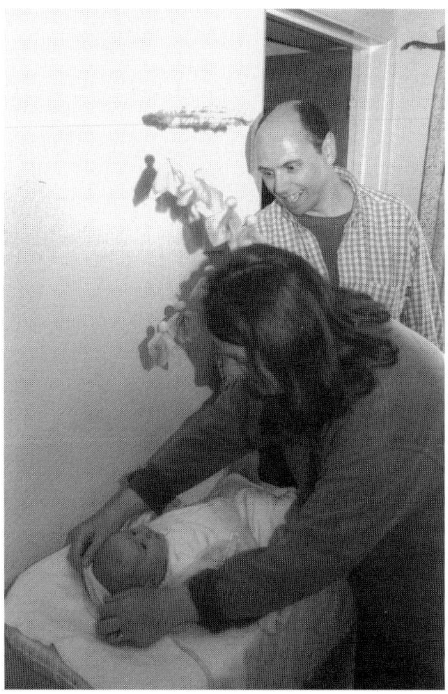

Marcus Webb and Cathy McQuillen with their new baby Annabelle Webb-McQuillen.

Jo Andreae

Jackie Livermore's children watch her prepare a meal. Jackie runs her own arts and crafts business from home.

Jo Andreae

A leisurely ride in Broad Lane.

June Dutton

Jo Fletcher moved to Bucklebury about 18 years ago and has been making cakes professionally for special occasions for 15 years.

Jo Andreae

Valerie Coulson, Byles Green, recaning a chair - another cottage industry.

Jo Andreae

Meri Mower runs her own garden and landscape business.

June Dutton

One of Jo Firth's pots.

Jo Andreae

Jo Firth, a potter at Burden's Heath, has practised the 16th century Japanese art of Raku for 10 years. Her work is exhibited nationally and sold internationally.

Jo Andreae

R & R Roofing.

Robin Jury, who has lived in Bucklebury all his life, started his business about 12 years ago. His sons Danny and Michael work with him.

Jo Andreae

R & R Roofing about to repair a roof.

The Barretts are an old Bucklebury family. Jim Barrett, Tony's father, ran the coal merchant's business in Long Grove and his brother, Victor, ran a shoe repair business in Broad Lane close to the Memorial Hall.

When Jim retired, Tony took over. He too retired in 1998, selling the business to Pinnocks in Thatcham. He didn't mention his impending retirement to his customers because he didn't think anybody would be interested. However, on his last day as he did his rounds the customers' comments and goodbyes brought tears to his eyes.

June Dutton

Tony Barrett in 1998.

Jo Andreae

Bob Millson opened a repair shop on The Corner Piece in his mother's garage. This expanded and his sons helped him for a time. Eventually the business was sold and this is it today, Kingfisher Car Sales. The Curridge Bodyshop is further to the right.

Updating our roads

In spring 1999 Little Lane was in a terrible state until it was resurfaced and the junction with Broad Lane was given new white lines.

Jo Andreae

Jo Andreae

Jo Andreae

Tarmacing Little Lane. 1999

Jo Andreae

The speed limit on the major roads through the parish, including here on Broad Lane, was changed from 40 to 30mph early in 1999.

Byles Green c1930. This end is locally known as the Ups and Downs.

Jo Andreae

Shirley and Roger Aylward with their son and dog out for a Saturday morning stroll. 1999

Jo Andreae

More cottages at Byles Green.

Jo Andreae

Burden's Heath used to be part of Thatcham. Consequently it is the only part of Bucklebury parish with street lights.

The Three Crowns public house

The Three Crowns and the cottage next door date from at least the 1750's.

Before the Three Crowns was sold to a Newbury brewery in the last century, it brewed its own beer like many small pubs. In the 1990's the business was sold and relaunched as Peppercorns restaurant. It is now the Cottage Inn restaurant and bar.

The Three Crowns earlier this century. The second from the right is William Paulin.

The Three Crowns before the houses were built on the other side of the road. c1952

Jo Andreae

The Cottage Inn in 1998.

June Dutton

The Cottage Inn. These interiors were taken in 1999.

June Dutton

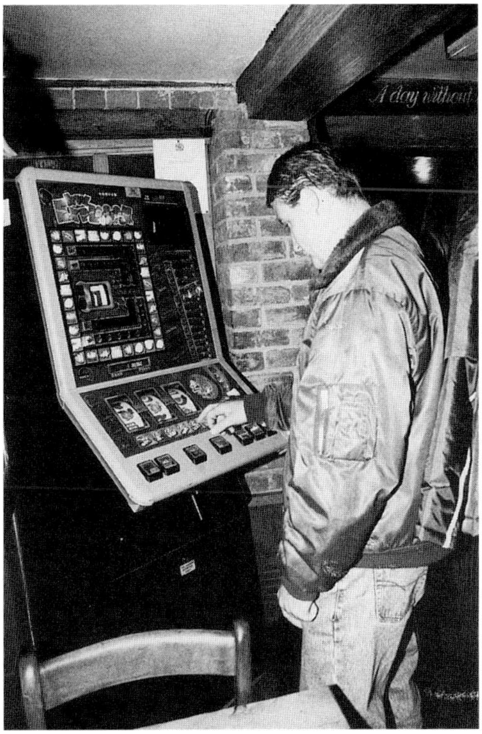

June Dutton

The Renaut family when they lived in this cottage in 1931. Later, the Cripps family lived here. The cottage was demolished in 1989.

Bucklebury Church of England Primary School

Jo Andreae

Coming to school on Monday morning in the minibus...

Jo Andreae

and going home again. 1998

June Dutton

Dawn Wilson, a former pupil of Bucklebury school, cooking the dinners in 1998. She attended the school in the village.

June Dutton

The school kitchen and entrance were added in the 1990's. The area in front of the school where the slide was, is now the outside classroom.

June Dutton

Classes in 1998

Computers have, during the last few years, become standard classroom equipment.

June Dutton

busily working

June Dutton

Top infants making fairground attractions in a design and technology lesson.

June Dutton

Practising!

June Dutton

Playing rounders in 1998.

June Dutton

Sports day in 1996.

June Dutton

At 8am on a Friday morning, Judo lessons are held.

June Dutton

In 1997 the local driving school owner, Nick Cornish, who had three children at the school, gave a new football strip to the team. It was inaugurated with a Driving School versus Primary School football match. The school won easily.

In the late 20th century, environmental education using school grounds has become important. Bucklebury parents started "The Green Team" and the children and adults meet after school. Their projects have included the outdoor classroom, a vegetable garden, a five continents flower garden and, in spring 1999, a pond.

June Dutton

The outdoor classroom.

A cycling proficiency training lesson on how to turn out of a side-road. Lessons are arranged by the school with a lot of voluntary help from the parents.

June Dutton

June Dutton

Colin Trembath, Chairman of Berkshire County Council, unveiled the plaque on completion of major building work. The oldest and youngest child in each class supported him. 1995

June Dutton

Fund raising. The winners of a Beetle drive in 1999.

Jo Andreae

Jumble sale in 1999.

June Dutton

The children paid for the privilege of wearing their red noses in school. In 1997 red noses were furry.

June Dutton

The school parents run a 200 club which celebrated its 10th birthday in 1997. To mark the occasion the draw was made at the Christmas Bazaar and Mrs Ann Evans received a cheque from Mrs Cornwell for £100. John Perry is on the right.

June Dutton

Christmas play in 1995.

June Dutton

Christmas play in 1997. Even the wall-bars in the hall were dressed up for the Christmas Nativity play and used as an escape route by the fleeing innocents.

June Dutton

The parents hold two Christmas parties; one for the younger children and one for the older ones. 1998.

June Dutton

The Christmas Bazaar had a Victorian theme (echoing the work done in history that term) but the customers showed a timeless appreciation of a sit-down with a cup of tea and a cake. 1998

June Dutton

The journey to Secondary school. A car ride to the bus stop followed by…

June Dutton

the bus.

All Saints Church

The foundation stone for the original All Saints church in Upper Bucklebury was laid in 1962. The wooden building is covered in cedar shingles.

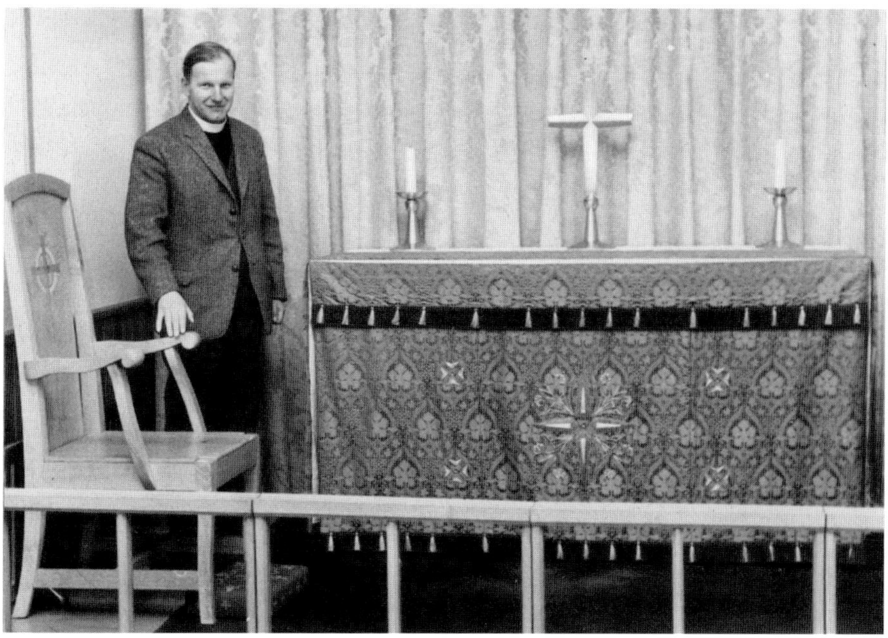

Rev David Ashburner at the original altar. Rosamund Carr made the altar cloth. 1965.

Jo Andreae

On Mothering Sunday the children give bunches of flowers to their mothers. April 1999

Jo Andreae

Mathematics and English adult education classes in the church hall.

The Bucklebury Wives' Group reunion on 28th March 1985 with former vicar Rev. Ashburner and present vicar Rev. Holmes holding the cake made by June Lawes. The group was founded by Mrs Ashburner in 1960. The few members left still meet once a month.

Jo Andreae

This extension was dedicated on 25th Jan 1988. The photograph was taken in 1999.

Marlston

St Mary's Church, Marlston has a Norman door and a 1607 sundial with the motto "Life as the shade doth fly and fade". The church was thoroughly restored in 1855 and in 1901 was renovated and enlarged by G.W. Palmer who lived at Marlston House.

Jo Andreae

St Mary's Church, Marlston, in 1998.

Jo Andreae

Marlston Cottages at the edge of the parish on a snowy winter's day, 1999.

Marlston Farm

Local mum gives advice

In 1946, Mrs Marchant, a mother of seven children, from Marlston Farm Cottages was one of ten housewives representing women's organisations invited to advise the government. They visited Whitehall and talked to Dr Edith Summerskill, Parliamentary Secretary to the Minister of Food about the new ration book design and food problems.

Stock prices in 1964

In October 1964, the Newbury Weekly News reported on the sale of farming stock from another local farm.

"Twenty months Hereford-cross Shorthorn heifers made £56, Shorthorn bulling heifers £50, served Jersey heifers £40 to £26, 12-months Hereford-cross Shorthorn steers and heifers (subsidy to come) £46 10s, yearling Friesian steers £40, Angus-cross ditto £35 10s, Angus-cross Friesian weaned calves £29 and Friesian-cross ditto £31 to £28."

Jo Andreae

The farm in 1999. The farm manager is Andy Crowhurst.

Jo Andreae

New and old buildings at Marlston Farm in 1999.

Brockhurst School

Marlston House, now Brockhurst School, was entirely rebuilt in 1895-9 by G.W. Palmer. He, along with Mr Huntley, ran the famous Huntley and Palmer's biscuit factory in Reading.

Brockhurst School in 1965.

Jo Andreae

Brockhurst School in 1999.

Jo Andreae

Serving dinner in 1999.

Jo Andreae

A lesson in Brockhurst School in 1999.

Turner's Green

Turner's Green takes its name from the bowl turners who worked here. Many local people in the past made their living from woodland crafts.

George Lailey (1869-1958) is our most famous bowl turner, sending his wooden bowls far and wide to be sold, even to Harrods in London. As his fame grew, people came to Bucklebury specially to buy his work.

Turner's Green showing the chapel and bowl turner's hut, before the Second World War.

To the right of this picture there is a chicken house surrounded by posts supporting a wire clothes line. This washing line belonged to the cottage opposite, once called Lavender Cottage, now replaced by Turner's Green House.

George Lailey worked with his father, William, at Miles's Green before the business moved to Turner's Green. Miles's Green House can just be seen in the middle of the picture.

An early picture of the bowl turner's hut at Turner's Green with a heap of logs ready for turning.

George outside his hut in the 1930's before it was reboarded.

George never married and first his mother, then his sister and finally his niece, Mary Matthews, looked after him. He lived his later years at Rest Harrow in Briff Lane. When George died in 1958, his tools were donated to the Museum of Rural Life in Reading where they form an impressive display.

A later picture of George working inside his hut. As a small boy, David Green remembers filling up several sacks with wood shavings and being rewarded with a few coppers for his efforts.

John Morton and the Congregational Chapel

John Morton was the famous farmer preacher who saved the Common from enclosure. He came with his widowed mother to live in Hope Cottage in the Slade as a boy and went to the Blue Coat School, Thatcham.

As a young man he became a member of the Congregational Chapel in Thatcham and then started preaching in the open air at Bucklebury. Later he held services in a disused blacksmith's shop on Turner's Green. He founded the Congregational Chapel which was built and opened in 1840 where he ministered for 56 years. John died in 1871.

The chapel still holds regular Sunday services.

John Morton.

Leaving the chapel after a "Pilots" meeting in the Sunday school in the 1960's.

The old kitchen, at the back of Turner's Green Chapel, was originally a stable. The preacher's horse was tethered here while he was taking the service.

Jo Andreae

Candlelit Service in the chapel, Christmas 1998

To celebrate the 50th anniversary of V.E. Day on May 1995, an exhibition of Bucklebury wartime memorabilia was held in the Chapel. Mrs B. Haines, centre left, is talking about the loss of her brother near the end of the Second World War.

Jo Andreae

The Rendalls at Apple Tree Cottage in 1999.

June Dutton

Rixson's pond, like others on the common, was used to water the animals belonging to the commoners. The Rixson family were bowl turners at Turner's Green.

Jo Andreae

Some people still grow their own fruit and vegetables. Here we see Margaret and Malcolm Wallis tending the grape vine and cucumbers in their greenhouse in the summer of 1999.

Jo Andreae

Hand ploughs like this were used by cottagers to till their soil well into the first half of the 20th century. Here are Bethany and Jonathan Kent, aged 10 amd 6 years old, with the old plough in 1999.

Jo Andreae

The Kent family, like a number of local people continue the tradition of keeping chickens to provide their family with new-laid eggs. Here Jonathan and Bethany are collecting the eggs.

The old crafts have gone to be replaced by new ones more appropriate to our times. The business 'A Cut Above The Rest' is a prime example of this. Jan Hayward started her business in 1996 as her children became more independent. She works from home as a hairdresser and curtain maker.

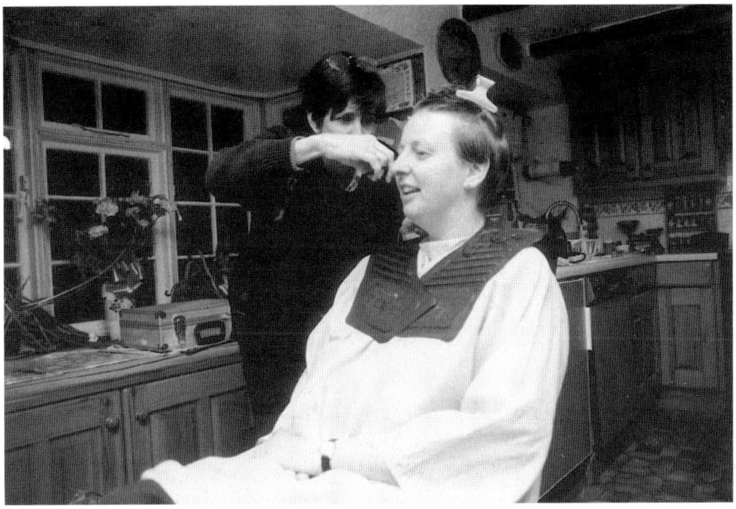

Jo Andreae

Jan in her kitchen in 1999 cutting Jo Andreae's hair .

Jo Andreae

Jan making curtains .

The Slade

The Slade showing the start of the City Path and Miss Edith Morton's cottage. Mr John Sellwood and his wife Ellen lived in Ferndale, the house at the end just before the car. c1913

Further down the road.
The dark shed in the front garden of the cottage was the wash house and shows the chimney of the copper that was used to boil the washing. Clothes props are leaning against the chimney.

The top of the Slade Road. c1910
The bracken rick at the base of the tree on the left is for animal bedding.

Jo Andreae

The same view in 1999.

A Baptist Chapel Sunday school outing in the mid 1930's.

John Morton, the farmer preacher who established the chapel in Turner's Green, had a son, also named John, who became a Baptist. He, along with two friends, Isaac Allum and Henry Coxeter, were baptised in the River Pang.

After he married he held services in his cottage and later in a portable wooden building in an orchard. A plot of land was bought and the chapel was moved there permanently. It was pulled up Slade Hill on wagon wheels by two heavy horses helped by the congregation pushing from behind.

Later, the cottagers managed to raise £100 for a new building which was erected around the wooden chapel so that services could continue.

The chapel closed in 1975. The building is pictured here in 1998.

June Dutton

The old Baptist chapel.

Mercy with her grandchildren.

Here is a picture of John Morton's daughter, Mercy, who married John Sellwood. Her son John, referred to at the beginning of this chapter, had four children, three of whom are seen here, Joseph, Violet and the youngest, Albert. Mary is not in the photograph.

This later picture shows Miss Edith Morton on the left with the Sellwood sisters, Mary and Violet.

Mary taught at Bucklebury School as a pupil teacher. Later she married Sidney Paulin and ran the little shop in the Slade for many years.

Mary, seated, with Edith and Violet.

Slade Farm c1910.

Slade Farm taken after Phillip Froude died. His dairy herd was often left to range all over the Common, the cows finding cottagers' garden plants particularly tasty!

Jo Andreae

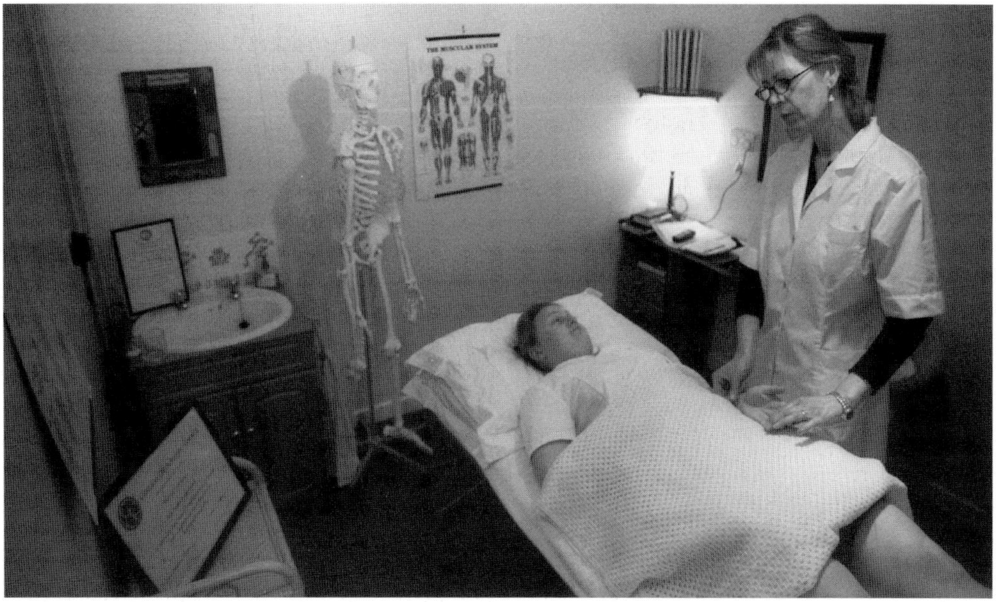

A session at Tiverton Clinic

Keith and Jennifer Parkes, with their daughter Sophie, started the Tiverton House Clinic in 1997. They provide complementary therapies, including osteopathy, homeopathy, acupuncture, aromatherapy and reflexology.

Jo Andreae

Hilary and Chas Cairns live in Hope Cottage and run their globe making business, World Globes, from the old Baptist Chapel. Components are imported, then married to bases and stands from a local wood turner. The globes are distributed throughout the UK, many into the education sector.

William Paulin in the 1920s.

William Paulin was a woodsman, working local copses in rotation, cutting one each year. His daughter, Joan Martin, remembers him cutting birch for the Thatcham turnery works to make into broom handles. He made ash hurdles six bars deep, working under the oak trees on the Top Green in the Slade. In 1920's and early 30's he was selling and delivering these for 6 pence each.

Brush wood was used to make 4 foot long "bavins" for heating bread ovens. Four sticks made a base and the brushwood was tied round it. They were just long enough to go in the bread oven. After they had burnt the ashes were raked out ready for the bread to be put in to bake. Ricks of bavins were made so that bakers could order them in the summer.

Other uses for the brush wood included birch "puffs" for the race course and for besoms, bean and pea sticks.

In winter the wood was cut and piled around the stumps to stop deer grazing the regrowth. Conservation volunteers who cut these much neglected copses to rejuvenate them now do the same.

William's father, John, served as a Hayward of the Common. His duties included moving gypsies on, and to "pound" any stray horses. There was a wooden pound in the Slade by the track beside Highcroft, though there is no trace of it now.

Like many commoners the Paulins grazed sheep on the Common and Joan can remember shepherding the sheep for her father.

William's flock grazing the Common.

Talbot Cottage in 1970.

Overdale was once home of Tom and Harriet Robbins. Their son, Henry P. Robbins, was born here in 1815. He married Ann Osgood, moved to Downhill, the Slade and then, in 1848 with their three small children, left for the USA.

Jo Andreae

John Morton, the farmer preacher, lived and farmed at Holly Farm. This picture was taken in 1999.

Jo Andreae

The pond opposite the farm house has been restored by the Pang Valley Countryside Project.

Where we live

Bucklebury, like many rural parishes, has changed dramatically during the last hundred years. Out of interest we looked at the 1900 electoral roll, remembering that this was before universal suffrage, and compared it with the 1999 electoral roll. In 1900 there were about 170 voting men and in 1999 there were 1679 voting adults.

When we started putting the pictures together for the book, we found they fell naturally into chapters relating to the different areas of Bucklebury. The population in 1900 and 1999 was distributed as you see below. You will notice that the proportion of photographs tends to follow the current population pattern, apart from The Village.

Area	**Homes 1900**	**Homes 1999**	**Photographs**
The Village	16%	8%	26%
Chapel Row and the Blade Bone	12%	17%	10%
The Avenue	15%	6%	4%
The Common	13%	12%	10%
Upper Bucklebury	16%	44%	36%
Marlston	7%	4%	2%
Turner's Green	4%	2%	7%
The Slade	17%	5%	5%

Sources and bibliographies

The Berkshire Weather Book – Ian Currie, Mark Davison & Bob Ogley, 1994
Bucklebury. A Berkshire Parish – A.L. Humphreys, 1932
Bucklebury and Marlston Women's Institute photograph albums
The Bucklebury Estate Sale Catalogue – 1922
Bucklebury's Heritage – Cecilia Millson, revised edition 1994
The History of Donnington Hospital – Cecilia Millson, 1985
Kelly's Directory – 1906 & 1935
Newbury Weekly News

Willie Hartley Russell – private archives
Sue Hopson – private archives

front cover - photograph by Jo Andreae
back cover - photograph by June Dutton
title page – view of The Avenue, 1999. Photographer Jo Andreae.
verso of title page – George Lailey finishing off handled bowls. Newspaper cutting.
iii – St Mary's Church, Bucklebury, postcard. P.O. Collier, early 1900's.